BOUNDARIES AND LANDMARKS

A PRACTICAL MANUAL

BY

A. C. MULFORD

ILLUSTRATED

NEW YORK

D. VAN NOSTRAND COMPANY

25 PARK PLACE

1912

ISBN: 978-0-359-07837-0

PREFACE.

THIS manual is intended to familiarize the surveyor with the different types of old boundaries that exist throughout the country. A great deal has been written on this general subject, especially in reference to the public lands of the West. Very little, however, is being done on the conveyances of the Eastern States, and it is my hope to furnish something which may prove useful to those who are likely to meet with cases of this sort. No attempt is made to describe how the lines should be measured; the intent is rather to furnish suggestions as to the method of locating the line to be measured — in short, finding it. It is far more important to have faulty measurements on the place where the line truly exists, than an accurate measurement where the line does not exist at all.

A. C. M.

NEW YORK,
Sept., 1912.

CONTENTS.

Boundaries and Landmarks

CHAPTER I.

THE WORK AND TRAINING OF THE SURVEYOR.

As compared with the vocation of the civil engineer, the calling of the surveyor has always been regarded as comparatively easy and simple. This is true not only in the popular conception of the two lines of work, but also in the view taken of them in text-books and in courses of instruction. The training of the surveyor consists essentially in practice in turning angles, measuring lines and getting over obstructions, to which are added rather meager suggestions on the subjection of the compass and the re-running of old surveys. He is considered preëminently a measurer of land. This is very true, and in certain localities and under certain conditions this may compose almost the entire work of the surveyor. But in the vast majority of cases the actual measuring of land forms the smaller portion of his duties. His hardest work is often, to use a colloquial phrase, to " find the land " to be surveyed.

In a large part of our land, through the generations past, the precise boundaries of holdings have received little attention. In the years when land was worth comparatively little, when there was little money to be spared from the necessities of life for surveys, and when the surveys, when made, were very crude, little attention was given to the establishment or the maintenance of boundaries. Loose, faulty and ignorant conveyances, the use of perishable landmarks or no landmarks at all, the temptation to build fences " off line " for a dozen reasons, good and bad, and innumerable other things have conspired to render the boundaries of land the most uncertain of all things.

We have to-day fully entered upon the era of high land values. The high prices paid by the wealthy for lands from which to form estates have revolutionized the methods of handling realty. The title of all property must be absolutely guaranteed and payment is usually made by the acre. As a result heavy demands are made upon the surveyor who finds himself confronted by two necessities, first, the necessity of making an extremely accurate set of measurements and, secondly, the necessity of defining clearly the boundaries of the land which he must measure — and the latter is by far the harder task. These problems he must work out single-handed and with the fear of failure shadowing him day by day and hour by hour. Since no two problems present exactly the same complications, it is useless for any one to attempt to lay out any fixed rules of procedure, yet it may be fairly said that from experience each surveyor acquires a certain amount of definite information concerning boundaries and landmarks and certain definite conceptions concerning the relative importance of different kinds of evidence, both direct and circumstantial. He is compelled to formulate for his own use certain general methods of procedure, and it is probable that the methods worked out by different surveyors bear a much closer resemblance to each other than would be supposed at first thought.

As far as my observation goes, in his preparatory studies the surveyor receives little help or suggestion to enable him to grapple with this important but elusive part of his work. The intention of this treatise is to endeavor to meet, in a small and tentative manner, this very distinct need. A good deal has been written on this general subject with reference to the public lands of the West, but little has been done in this line in connection with the ordinary conveyances of the eastern United States. My hope is to furnish something which may prove useful to those who are destined to wrestle with problems of this nature. No attempt will be made to describe methods of measuring the line; the intention is to furnish suggestions for finding the line which is to be measured. For after all, when it comes to a question of the stability of property and the peace of the community, it is far more important to have a somewhat faulty measurement of the spot where the line truly exists than it is to have an extremely accurate measurement of the place where the line does not exist at all.

CHAPTER II.

THE DESCRIPTION OF PROPERTY. SIMPLE DEEDS WITHOUT DIMENSIONS.

THE description of property by landmarks and by boundaries is very ancient. A special curse is pronounced in the Old Testament against the man who shall remove his neighbor's landmark, while a very large part of the Book of Joshua is occupied by the description of the various pieces of land allotted to the different houses of the Israelites. While the chief importance was put on the landmark, yet it is plain that there was felt a need of some further concrete description of the land. This feeling has increased with the growth of civilization, until to-day we have arrived at the guaranteed title and the detailed map which accompanies it. The need of such descriptions is intensified by the habitual ignorance of boundaries which is to be found in those who have occupied land for many years. Every surveyor has had numberless cases where the owners have been absolutely unable to follow out the boundaries of their land even approximately, and equally numerous cases where boundaries pointed out in all confidence and certainty have been found to be grossly inaccurate. A written description on the other hand, while it may be originally faulty and while it is liable to clerical error in

4

copying, is free from the personal equation — it is free from preconceived ideas and it does not forget with the lapse of years.

The surveyor, then, is driven at once to supplement and correct the personal information furnished him by every-thing in the way of recorded descriptions on which he can lay his hands.

These records are of three kinds:

1. Records of the piece of land in question.

2. Records of the private lands which bound it.

3. Records of the public lands which bound it, in the form of highways, etc.

To the above boundaries should perhaps be added bound-aries by water, were it not for the fact that boundaries by water are from their shifting nature essentially without the established records found in the three previous cases. The law prescribes clearly the course to be followed in surveying along water boundaries.

The records of the land in question and of the private lands adjoining are, of course, the deeds which conveyed the properties to their owners. These deeds are to be found in the hands of the owners or in certain places where they have, for one reason or another, deposited them. Cer-tified copies of them are also to be found (unless the deed has gone unrecorded), fully indexed, in the Office of the County Clerk, where they are open to public inspection. To these records must be added such former maps and "cards of land" as may have been made and preserved.

They are a great help when they can be obtained, but they are usually few and far between.

The records of the public lands adjoining are usually records of Town Highways or County Highways, to be found with the Town and County clerks respectively. In the case of municipal surveys there are records of streets, parks, etc., which are to be found with the proper city officials.

The fundamental description of property, however, is to be regarded as the DEED, and it is necessary first to consider the nature and intention of this instrument in order to understand why it is so often disappointing and deficient from the surveyor's standpoint.

A deed is essentially a lawyer's not a surveyor's document. Its intention is to make the possession of a certain piece of land sure to the owner forever, not to give a minute description of the land for the comfort of the surveyor. For legal reasons some lawyers prefer to omit from a deed all data of direction and length of the boundaries, describing it only by adjoiners and landmarks or by adjoiners only. Such a deed, after stating the names of the seller and buyer, the amount of compensation, the date of the transfer and the town, county and state where the land is situated, would proceed to the description somewhat as follows:

" Beginning at the Northwest corner of the property to be conveyed where it adjoins the Highway leading from M—— to N—— and running thence in an Easterly direction along the land of William Smith until it comes to the land of Richard Jones, thence, in a Southerly direction along the land of the said Richard Jones to a large stone at the Southeast corner of the land being conveyed where it adjoins the land of Richard Jones and land now or late of John Brown, thence in a Westerly direction along the land now or late of John Brown to the East side of the aforesaid Highway, thence in a Northerly direction along the Easterly side of the aforesaid Highway to the point or place of beginning, Containing within the said bounds Forty and one-half acres of land be the same more or less."

Then usually follow references to the records of earlier transfers of the same land, showing continuity of title and various other matter according to the particular nature of the deed. Finally come the signatures of the grantors, the acknowledgment before a Notary Public and the County Clerk's memorandum of public record.

It is argued that the above description clearly and concisely conveys all the land lying in the four-sided area bounded by Smith, Jones, Brown and the highway without raising any questions or controversies; while if directions and distances were given they might fall short of or overlap the known boundaries of the adjoiners, in one case leaving unclaimed gores of land and in the other leading to boundary controversies. Nevertheless, the surveyor is expected to take this deed and from it define the land with the greatest clearness and accuracy.

It is probable and it may be fairly said that there are

two standpoints from which the surveying of the above piece of land may be regarded. In the first place this land may be surveyed " as occupied " or " as found in possession." This means that it is to be surveyed according to the present standing boundaries between the land and its four adjoiners, no attempt being made to raise the dangerous question as to whether the fences, etc., occupy to-day the original boundary lines. If this method is satisfactory to all parties interested, there seems to be no reason why the land should not be measured and marked as the boundaries stand. But to guard against complications in the years to come, the map or description should be clearly marked " surveyed as occupied " or " surveyed as found in possession " or " as the fences now stand " and the date given. This will prevent misunderstandings which might arise from the survey being subsequently used to settle boundary disputes.

The other method, which is generally adopted as the correct one, is to endeavor to determine the boundaries of the land " as originally intended to be conveyed." In eight cases out of ten all parties would prefer to get back to the original boundaries as they stood at the time of the early transfers. This is all the more desirable since the deed made out yesterday is very apt to follow closely, or verbatim, the wording of the early descriptions. In cases of boundary controversies this method must always be followed. In any case it does no harm to know the ancient conditions, since it is a very simple matter for all the parties concerned to set aside the old boundaries in favor of the new, if they believe this to be the wiser course.

For this reason throughout this treatise it will be taken for granted that the surveyor is trying to get back to the boundaries of the land "as originally intended to be conveyed."

CHAPTER III.

THE RELATIVE LEGAL VALUE OF EVIDENCES OF BOUNDARY.

THE description in the preceding chapter may be regarded as fairly representing that very large class of descriptions in which no dimensions are given but where the land is described by adjoiners and landmarks. Therefore it is manifest that the decisions of the surveyor must be based on two kinds of evidence only:

1. Landmarks in the field.
2. The claims of the adjoiners.

The subject of landmarks must be taken up in detail separately, while the same laws which govern the description of the land in question will also apply to the descriptions of the adjoiners' lands.

Before going farther it may be well to note briefly the order of importance which the law assigns to the different kinds of evidence which come under the cognizance of the surveyor.

In a book entitled " The Law of Operations Preliminary to Construction in Engineering and Architecture " by John Cassan Wait, M.C.E., LL.B (John Wiley & Sons, 1900), the author has taken up very fully from a legal standpoint the problems of the surveyor. A few quotations from the chapter entitled " Description. Conflict of Calls " throw much light on the relative value of the evidence in question. Mr. Wait says:

"The calls as generally adopted to locate a survey are in the following order, viz.: (1) monuments or marks on the ground; (2) calls for adjoiners; (3) courses and distances; (4) quantity or area. If the marks found upon the ground conflict with the calls for adjoiners, with the courses and distances, and with the area, the marks upon the ground, i.e., the monuments, must still govern.

"The monuments themselves need not exist, for where they are gone they may be supplied by proofs of their former existence.

"The rule is well established that where land is described by courses and distances, and also by calls for adjoiners, the latter will govern if there be a discrepancy and there are no monuments.

"The third factor in order of importance is the course, which is usually held to govern the distance.

"As quantity or area is directly dependent on courses and distances, being calculated from them, it should be controlled by them."

Under the general head of Marks in the Field the same author says:

"The highest and best evidence of the location of a tract of land is that furnished by the monuments found on the ground and which have been made for that particular tract.

"The line originally run, fixed and marked is the true

boundary line that will control irrespective of any mistakes or errors in running and marking the line.

" The marks on the ground of an old survey, indicating the lines originally run, are the best evidence of the location of the survey.

" The position of old fences may be considered in ascertaining disputed boundaries. As between the old boundary fences and any survey made for the monuments after dispute, the fences are by far the better evidence of what the lines of the lot actually were."

The first duty of the surveyor in running out a description without dimensions must therefore be to look for

1. Landmarks especially named for the piece of land in question, such as the " large stone " in the foregoing description;

2. The marks of a previous survey;

3. Indications of old fences.

If he cannot find sufficient evidence in one or more of these classes he should take up the claims of adjoiners, and if these again prove insufficient for locating the line he should urge all parties interested to settle upon a new boundary line by common agreement. But the search for the landmarks must come first.

CHAPTER IV.

LANDMARKS.

STAKES AND STONES.

CERTAIN landmarks may be specifically mentioned in a description. These may perhaps be called special landmarks and must be identified as far as possible from the characteristics named in that description. But beside these there are a large number of general marks not mentioned perhaps in the deed, but which are nevertheless of the greatest possible value. Yet there can be no hard and fast classification of these, because they vary greatly with locality. On Long Island, where the most of my own work lies, there are certain marks which are of the highest importance, yet their use is confined largely, if not entirely, to Long Island. From the great abundance of yellow locust and the great capacity of its wood for resisting decay, it is used almost exclusively for surveyors' stakes in this section. "To a locust stake" is the typical phrasing of a Long Island description. It is preëminently the surveyor's mark for the locality, yet it is manifestly not a landmark for regions where the yellow locust does not grow. For the reason that stones of glacial origin are plentiful in the hills of the North Shore and scarce on the plains of the center and the South Shore the interpretation of the meaning of stones as indicating old boundaries differs considerably in localities actually separated by perhaps only a dozen miles. The nature of landmarks or, more accurately speaking, of the marks employed to indicate a boundary, may therefore vary greatly with the locality, and it is imperative that the surveyor should at once familiarize himself with the usages which prevail in the section where he is working. There are, however, certain kinds of landmarks which are widespread in their general use, though local custom may modify even these somewhat. The following may be regarded, I think, as the most important:

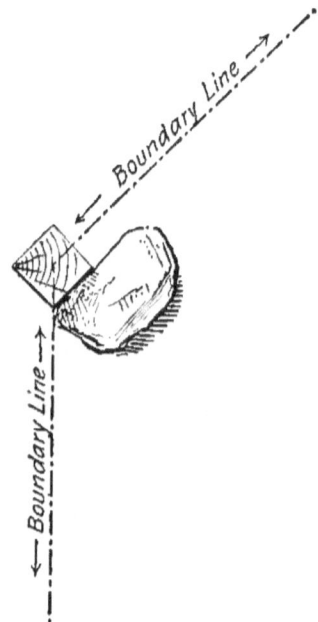

FIG. 1.   Stake and stone corner.

The stake. — A stake of some sort, driven down to mark a corner or a point where the course breaks, is one of the most universal landmarks. Besides the " corner stakes " one or more " line stakes " are frequently driven at different points on a long straight line to assist in following its direction.

Stake and stone. — A stake is often reinforced and emphasized by having a stone laid beside it, as shown by Fig. 1.   Sometimes there is a stone placed on either side, as shown by Fig. 2, and at times there are found four stones placed symmetrically around a stake, like in Fig. 3.   Sometimes there is a little irregular pile, as shown

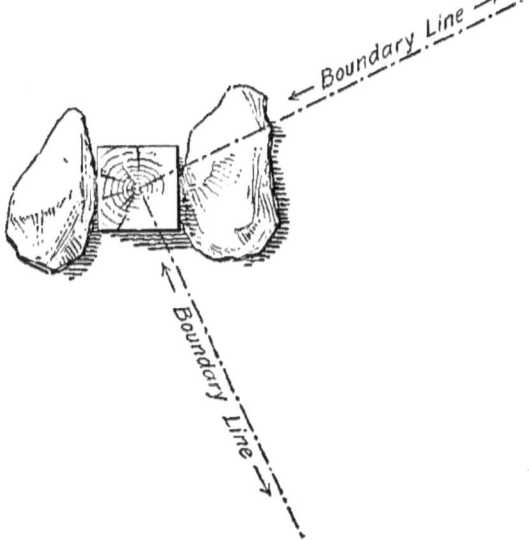

FIG. 2. Stone placed on either side of the stake.

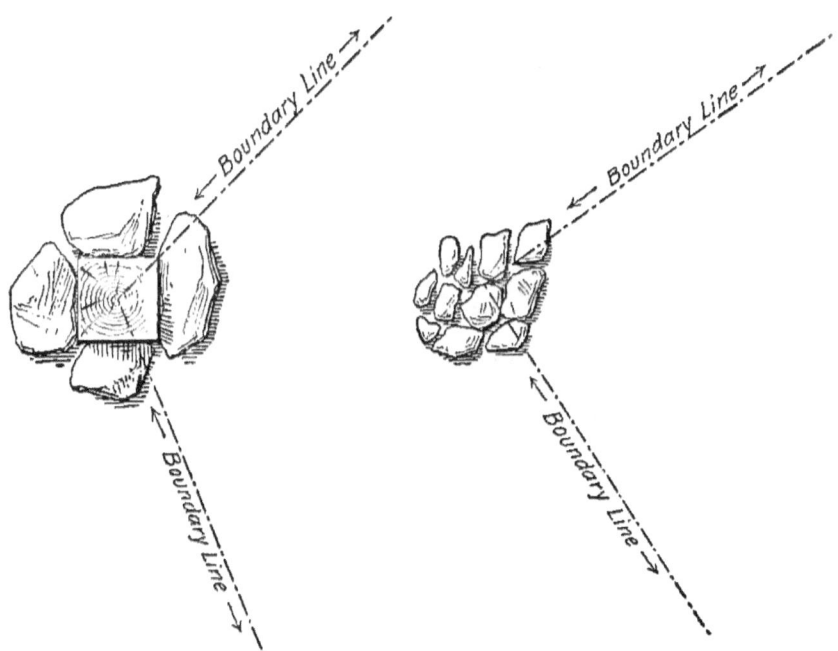

FIG. 3. Four stones placed sym- FIG. 4. Irregular pile of stones used
metrically around a stake.   for a corner.

by Fig. 4. The stone and stake are more frequently used at prominent angles of a piece of land, shown by Fig. 1. There seems to be little question that in these cases the stake is the actual corner — the stone simply emphasizes it.

The stone. — A stone set up for a landmark is a very ancient way of defining land, but like many ancient customs it is very vague. In sections where large stones are so scarce as to make them valuable for marks, a common custom is to place the stone or heap of stones squarely on the corner. The center seems to be the angle point. Such a large stone frequently defines a corner in unfenced land (Figs. 1 and 5).

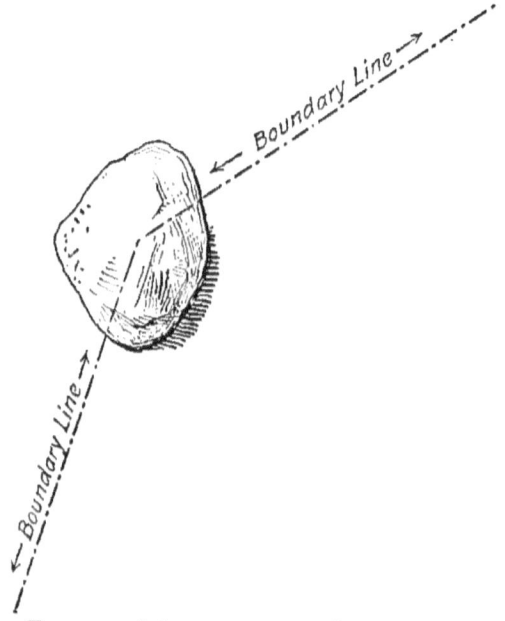

FIG. 5.   A large stone used as a corner.

In other places, more usually in fenced land, there are stones used as markers in a very different way. In these cases the owner of a piece of land selects a large stone having two faces meeting at approximately the same angle as do the two courses which join at the corner which he intends to mark. He then places the stone *entirely on his own land*, fitting the angle of the stone into the angle of the courses, so that the two faces coincide with these courses

— Fig. 6 shows such a case. In case a stone with suitable faces cannot be found or in case the angle is of more than 180 degrees, he frequently takes a stone with one strong angle and places this angle coincident with the point of junction of the courses, as you will see by Fig. 7. Where well-marked fences are still standing it is easy to interpret this corner. Sometimes the stone is so happily shaped that the meaning is clear, but where there is the slightest trace of doubt, prompt inquiry should be made

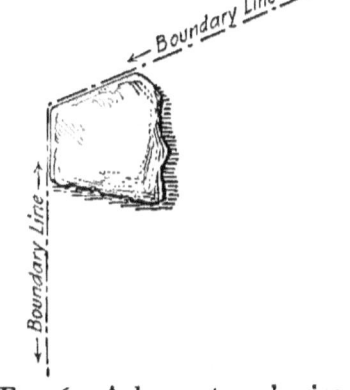

FIG. 6. A large stone having two faces, meeting at approximately the same angle, as do the courses that join at that point.

as to who originally placed the stone. As far as the author has been able to observe, these stones present some or all of the following characteristics: (1) they possess one particularly conspicuous angle, (2) they have every appearance

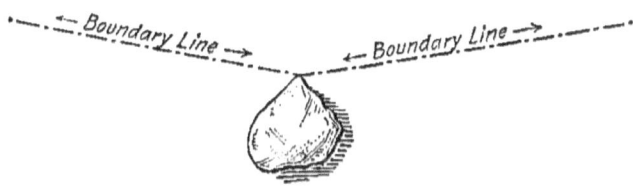

FIG. 7. A sharp pointed stone placed at the junction of the courses.

of having been placed artificially, (3) they are usually on end or on edge. The presence of these characteristics will generally suggest when this form of marking has been used, though the common corner stone may sometimes present some of the same characteristics. These private angle stones have been mistaken for common corner stones and the station made over the center, where there was no possible doubt that it should have been made at the edge. In such cases the surveyor should collect all the evidence he can and then decide in favor of the balance of probability.

Fence stones. — There is one other class of stones which is to be found in some sections and which is of the greatest importance. Reference is made to the so-called " fence stones." In certain sections the oldest fences were almost invariably of the zigzag rail type known as " worm," " snake " or " Virginia rail." Under the apex of each zigzag, where the ends of the rails crossed, it was the custom to place a stone in order to raise the lower rail from the ground and prevent its decay. This is particularly true on Long Island. The old fences have long since disappeared and new fences have been erected in their place, or it may be that hedgerow and forests have reclaimed their own; but there the ancient stones lie in two parallel rows, the individuals of one row alternating with those of the other. The line always ran down the center of such a fence and therefore now lies midway between these two parallel lines of stones. The points at which the line breaks are to be found by ranging out the rows, the course changing where the range of the fence stones changes. It should be remembered, however, that where these stones lie on steep earth hillsides they have a tendency to slide

down hill. Also there are few people who have the ability
to "line a fence" straight
across hill and hollow. So
it not unfrequently hap-
pens that where an old map
or survey shows unmistak-
ably one long straight
course, the fence stones
may show half a dozen
short ones, the average
being identical.

The value of the fence
stones cannot be over-
estimated and the illustration, Fig. 8, will at once
show the conditions. Once
I was called upon to survey
an old farm which had ac-
quired value and was to be
sold by the acre. There
existed a good map of the
land made early in the last
century, but at different
times small tracts had been
purchased and added to
the farm while in other
portions of it sections had
been sold off, so that the boundaries were very uncertain.

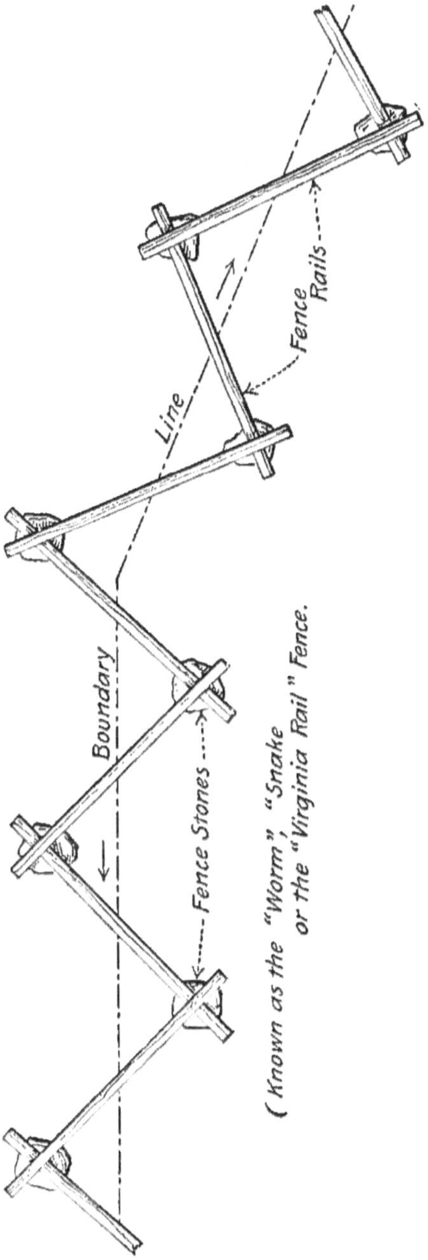

Fence Rails

Line

Boundary

Fence Stones

(Known as the "Worm", "Snake
or the "Virginia Rail" Fence.

FIG. 8.

Along the back line for about 700 feet the fences had
entirely disappeared, the wood had been
cut off and after the axe had come the
fires. The whole had " come up again
to sprouts." The owner, who had been
born on the land, twice endeavored to
show me the line. The second time he
got lost and, when he found himself,
was half a mile distant from the farm
itself. At last one fence stone was found
about where the line should be, then a
second and then a third in close prox-
imity. These gave the direction in
which to work. Finally, by searching
at the proper intervals, digging away
the mold here and prodding with a
range marker there, nearly every stone
of the series was found. Finally, when
the survey was plotted, it was found
that the fence stones marked the original
back line of the old map, the only
difference being that the map gave one
long straight course and the fence stones
six or seven short courses (Fig. 9 shows
the conditions). In searching for fence
stones it should be remembered that the
rows are usually about four feet apart
and that the rails which they supported were twelve feet

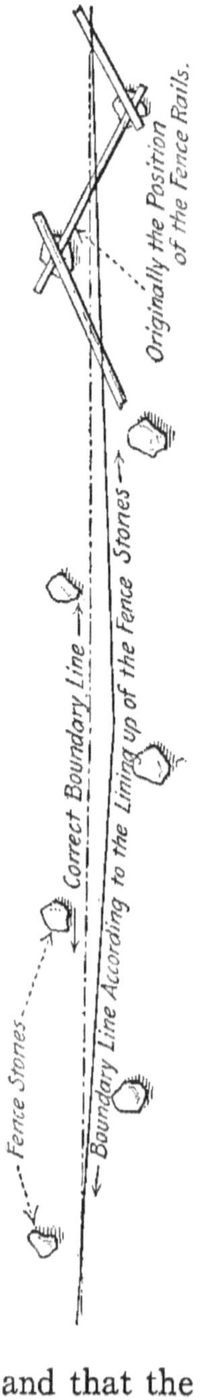

FIG. 9. Originally the position of the fence rails.

in length. In some cases I found that old fence stones
were removed to be used for other
purposes. The holes, however,
which were left in digging them
out, will often mark their former
location for some years.

Fence stones are almost always
landmarks of long standing, for while
new rails are often laid on the old
stones, it is doubtful if this form of
fence is ever erected along new lines
at the present time, — the post-and-
rail fence and the wire fence have
succeeded it,—and the zigzag fences
now standing probably represent
later erections on old foundations.

In determining the point where
fences of this sort come together at
an acute angle, care should be taken
to extend the ranges of the two
fences to their logical intersection,
as it is a very common practice to
join the rails across from one line to
the other before the actual point of
intersection is reached.

In conclusion it may be fairly
said that in the fence stones you
have not one or two boundary stones but a consecutive

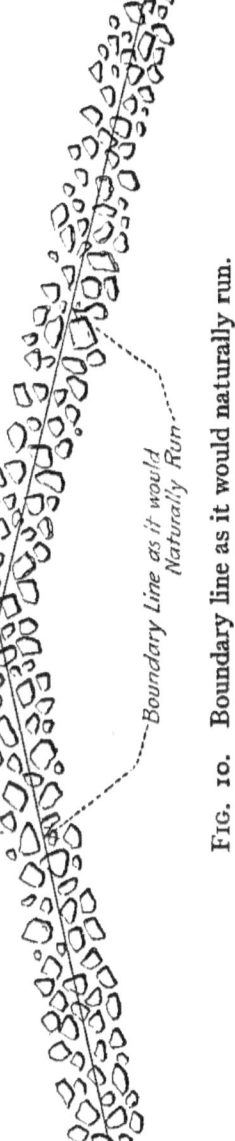

FIG. 10. Boundary line as it would naturally run.

Boundary Line as it would Naturally Run

series so numerous that the loss of a number of members
makes no essential difference.   I have found them to be
universally considered landmarks so ancient and so clear
that controversy might not extend beyond them.   If the
fence stones were found, all the parties concerned were
completely satisfied.

There is one other arrangement of stones which may be
regarded as a very good landmark.   It is a common custom to throw the small waste stones picked up on cultivated fields under the fences which border these fields.
These collections of stones often furnish an excellent
method of determining the *general* location of a long van-
ished fence, as you will see by Fig. 10.   The belt which
they occupy is often several feet wide and they may originally have been thrown only on one side of the fence;
but they are often of the very greatest service in determining the approximate position of a boundary line.   They
must not be confounded with the " fence stones " among
which they may lie.

CHAPTER V.

LANDMARKS (continued).

MARKED TIMBER. DITCHES AND BALKS.

TREES are frequently used as monuments in the description of property. In these cases the kind of tree is usually named or the tree is specified as a " marked " tree. As far as the author's personal experience goes, he has found that in the sections where stone for landmarks was scarce, extra attention was given to marking or " blazing " the trees. In the southern portion of Long Island, for instance, there are few fence stones but there is a good deal of marked timber.

The methods of marking timber to indicate a line must of necessity vary greatly with locality and usage, but there are certain " blaze marks " which are so well established that they must be regarded as extremely important, especially as they usually come under the head of " marks on the ground of an old survey." A property owner often sets up the artificial landmarks, but it is more frequently the surveyor who marks the timber.

Corner trees. — A " corner tree " is usually marked in some distinctive way (Fig. 11 shows one). Sometimes a series of three notches, one over the other, is cut on each of the four sides, or it may be that these notches are con-

Fig. 11. The three notches in some cases are cut on the four sides of the tree, and in other cases, only on one side when the intersecting lines enter the tree.

Fig. 12. The stone being jammed into the roots of the tree, where it enters the ground.

fined to the sides where the intersecting lines enter the tree. Sometimes a stone is jammed into the earth at the foot of the tree to emphasize the corner, like in Fig. 12. There is an instance where the stump of a corner tree which had been small and inconspicuous had been cut down

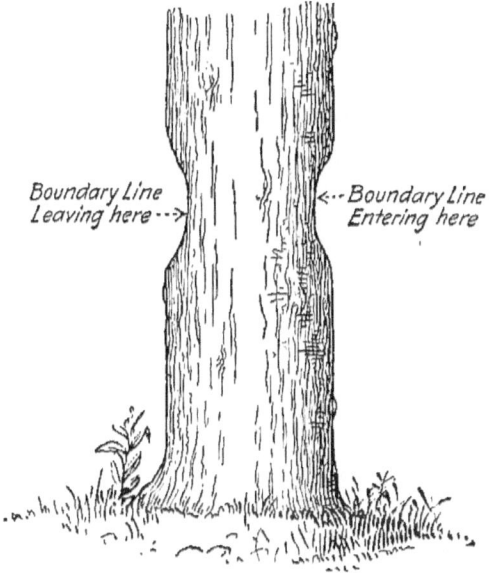

Boundary Line Leaving here -->   <-- Boundary Line Entering here

FIG. 13.   Being a line tree a chip is taken out of opposite sides.

but the stone jammed in by the stump, especially as it was common local usage, identified it with certainty (see Fig. 12.)

Line trees. — A " line tree," i.e., a tree through which the line passes, is usually designated in the field by one of several ways. Ordinarily a liberal chip is cut out of the tree several feet above the ground at the point where the line enters it and another on the opposite side at the point where the line leaves it (Fig. 13 shows such a case). Sometimes a second pair of chips is cut out in such a way that the line connecting them is at right angles to the line of the survey, the tree thus being blazed on four sides. This arrangement has been found less frequent than the other. There are cases where you will find a line tree with only the second pair of chips removed. For lack of a better name any mark intended to indicate a line tree might be termed a " line blaze."

Lopped trees. — A friend of the author's who was an antiquarian as well as a surveyor, once called his attention

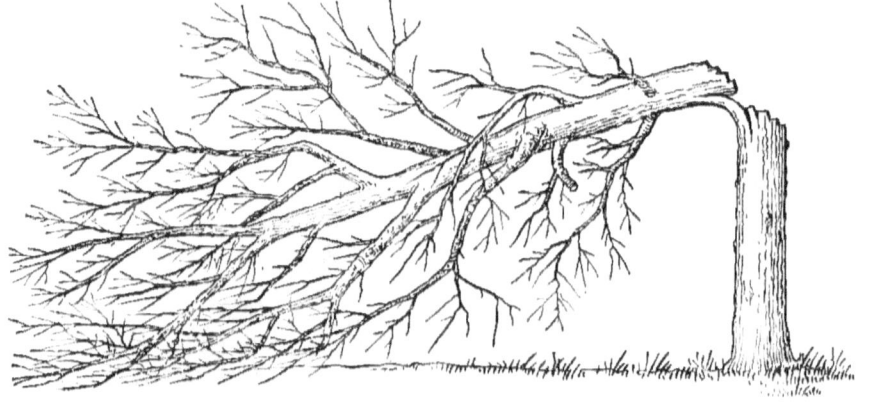

Fig. 14. A lopped tree, bent in the general direction of the boundary line.

to another very old form of line mark which he called a " lopped tree " (see Fig. 14). It seems that many old surveyors had a practice of " lopping " a sapling which came on the line, i.e., at a point several feet above the ground they cut the sapling half through in such a way that it could be bent over parallel to the ground and in the direction of the line. Such a sapling did not die nor did it ever become erect again. Though it might grow to great size, the main trunk was always horizontal or at least showed a double crook. The position of this trunk may indicate half a century later the location and general direction of the line of the early survey.

Another form of blaze is used on a tree that stands very close to the line though not actually on it. This mark

FIG. 15. Side line blaze.

consists in a chip taken out of the side of the tree which is next to the line. For lack of a better name this may be called a "side-line blaze" (see Fig. 15).

Of all these marks the "line-tree" blaze is the most valuable. It is usually strong and unmistakable. But all blaze marks must be treated with a certain amount of skepticism. A man clearing up a piece of woodland frequently places a side-line blaze on the trees which stand just over the line on his neighbor's land. Such marks are usually very nearly accurate for the reason that, unless the line was very clear, the man who was cutting the wood would not dare to define it. Scars looking very much like blaze marks may be formed on trees from natural causes, while it must be remembered that a small boy with a hatchet can mark up more trees in one Saturday afternoon than a dozen surveyors can in a year.

In general, blaze marks are to be regarded as suggestive and corroborative rather than determinative. They may suggest that the line runs in a place where you did not expect it and a subsequent study of the records may entirely confirm this. Or in a case where it has been necessary to render a decision on meager evidence, the finding of blaze marks may confirm the decision. But, in general practice, to render a definite opinion on the evidence of a few rather obscure blaze marks is, to say the least, rash. It must, however, be clearly understood that these remarks do not refer to the government blaze marks on public lands, these being clearly and carefully made. These remarks apply only to the cases met with in ordinary country surveying.

Ditches. — Ditches are frequently used to mark boundary lines, but usually in meadow lands only. In such cases the line, which usually runs down the center of the ditch, is frequently marked additionally by a stake at either end of the ditch or by a line of stakes extending from one end to the other. Such ditches are usually specifically mentioned in descriptions and their meaning is thereby made clear.

Balks. — The using of this term, which is of perhaps too local a nature, is meant in a wholly tentative manner. It is intended to signify all ridges of earth which mark a boundary line, whether they be natural or artificial.

A balk is sometimes simply a low wall of earth built along a boundary line. In such cases the line runs along the center and, if there has been a previous survey, the stakes will be found on top of the mound. It is my impression that this form is most frequently employed where the boundary line follows the junction of marsh and upland.

There is a second form much more difficult of interpretation, where a ditch has been excavated and the earth thrown up in a low mound along one side. This form is not confined to marsh lands, but is sometimes seen in unfenced woodland and hill country and also on the plains here on Long Island. It is an ancient, cheap and permanent method of marking poor land. The great trouble with it is that there seems to be no rule to determine whether the ditch or the balk marks the line. There are cases of it being both ways. If the deed throws no light on the subject, the surveyor must look for other marks on the ground or must consult persons who are familiar with the land and its history. It is a case where additional evidence must always be sought.

A third form of balk is largely the work of nature. The plow is a great destroyer, and where the soil has been loosened by it year after year, nature removes the excess of earth in ways of her own. On the other hand, where man has left the soil alone, nature builds up its surface from plant waste and makes its texture firm by interlacing roots. For this reason the level of cultivated fields is gradually lowered, while, if there is a hedgerow between them, the surface of this undisturbed portion may actually become slightly raised. If, after this, the fields be allowed to lie fallow and the hedgerow be entirely cleared away, the position of the latter will nevertheless be marked in all probability by a low broad balk, an ineradicable mark of ancient boundary.

After all has been said it must be fairly admitted that these three classes of landmarks, — blazed trees, ditches and balks, — though capable of very varied interpretation, form a most useful and valuable portion of the general body of evidence.

CHAPTER VI.

LANDMARKS (concluded).

FENCES AND WALLS.

IT is needless to say that walls and fences are of great importance as landmarks; nevertheless they do not prove to be such definite ones as would appear at first sight. It is very easy to say, " The fence is the line," but the question immediately rises — " *Whereabouts* in the fence is the line? " — and the same question may be asked concerning walls. This is a case where every effort should be made to find out the local usage, and the surveyor should not hesitate to consult the proper authorities — the carpenters who build the fences and the masons who lay the walls. These people are in the habit of doing their work from surveyors' stakes and they *should* be able to give *one* exact information in regard to how the fence was built, though they often fail.

The following rules, though they should be confirmed by consulting local usage, may be regarded as of very general application.

Fences and walls between adjoiners. — In rail fences of all kinds the line runs down the middle, half of the fence being on the land of one party and half on that of the other (see Fig. 16).

In wire fences the wires themselves are on line, the posts being entirely on the land of one party (see Fig. 17).

In picket fences and board fences two kinds of con-

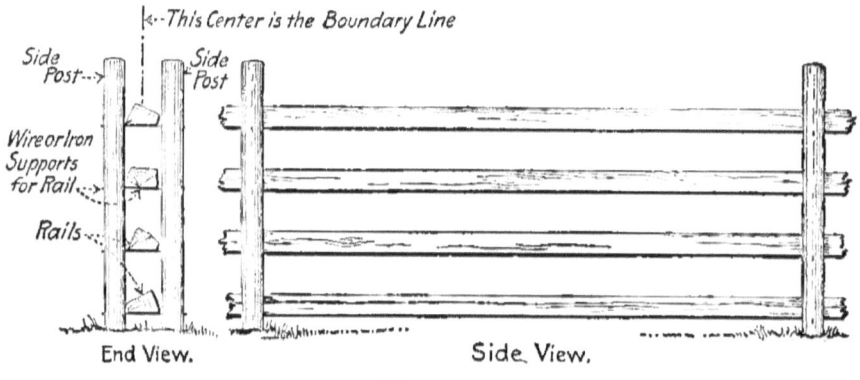

FIG. 16.

struction are found. In the first kind (see first case, Fig. 18), the battens or flat strips to which the pickets or boards

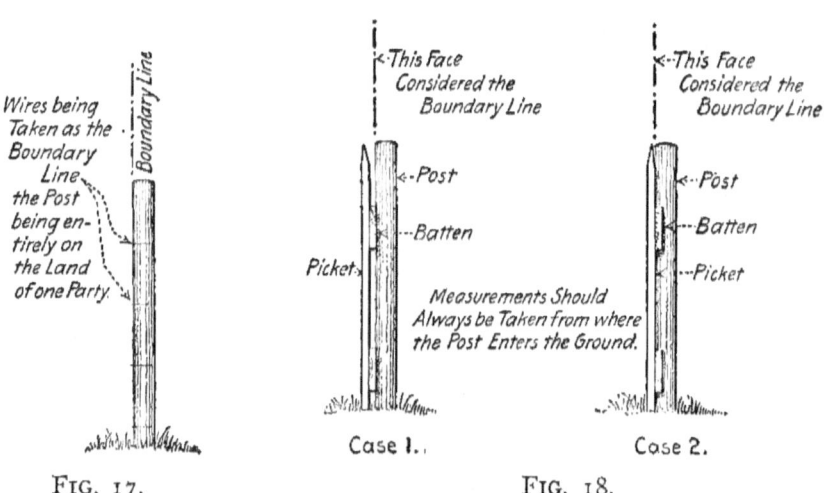

FIG. 17.　　　　　FIG. 18.

are nailed are fastened to the front of the posts; in the second (see second case, Fig. 18), the battens are sunk to their full depth in the face of the posts. In the former class the line where the posts and battens join is commonly considered the line, or in other words the front of the posts is the line, the posts being on the land of one party and the battens and pickets (or boards) on that of the other. In the latter class the front of the posts (or the back of the pickets) is still the line, but in this case both the posts and battens are on the land of one party and only the pickets on the other.

In fences composed only of a series of rows of battens nailed to the front of posts, the front of the posts or the back of the battens is the line, as shown by Fig. 19.

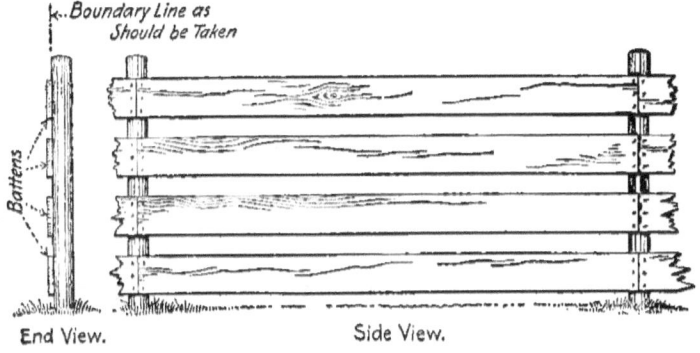

FIG. 19.

In all cases the measurements should be taken, not from the upper part of the post but from the point *where it enters the ground*. In case the post leans, the measurements should be taken from the point where the face of the post would enter the ground if the post were straightened up. As a general rule the posts at the ends of a fence are more nearly correct, since almost all fences are originally placed on line at their ends, though they frequently depart far from the course of rectitude before they reach the middle. Sometimes, however, in cases where the posts have sagged a good deal an average of the bottoms of the faces of a number of posts will be more nearly the true line than anything else.

In stone walls the line may be regarded as running down the center, except in the case of bank walls. In these the exposed face will generally be found to be on or a little back from the line.

Fences and walls on highways. — Here, as in the case of division boundaries, the line may be considered as running down the center of all rail fences.

In wire fences the wires themselves are on the line while the posts are on private land.

In the case of picket and board fences there seems to be great uncertainty, different builders following different methods, each according to his own judgment rather than by fixed rule. The majority, as far as I have been able to find out, bring the outer edge of the trimming strip or " ribbon " to the street line, though I am confident that others place the face of the posts to the line. Those following the former practice claim that the fence should be entirely on private land, and some extend this practice even to fences between adjoiners — a serious departure from the best practice. Probably, if the truth were known, you would find that the builder seldom inquires into the matter, for the reason that most fences which are built in the country simply replace old fences. In such cases every effort is made to line the new posts exactly with the old, so that the ancient intention, whatever it may have been, shall still be carried out (see Figs. 16, 17, 18 and 19).

Much valuable information for a locality can be obtained by consulting men who have for many years handled real estate in the section in question. In any case the surveyor should make every effort to determine local usage or lack of usage, and he should then be governed by common sense.

The outer surfaces of a square unboxed post standing at a street corner may be regarded as agreeing with the street lines.

A bank wall is to be considered as on private property, its face being placed on the street line or a little back of it.

In case of ordinary stone walls local usage should be carefully ascertained.

The above rules are by no means to be considered as unvarying, but any surveyor will agree that they fall in closely with the lines of common practice everywhere. As said before, the surveyor should in all cases make certain of the practices which prevail in the section where he is working.

It is to be borne in mind that where walls and fences have been removed for any purpose, frequently sufficient fragments are left below ground to determine accurately the position of the original line. Careful search will frequently reveal these fragments, and the surveyor should so far familiarize himself with the various methods of construction that he can immediately determine what position these crumbling fragments actually bear to the original line. Quite frequently on the removal of an old fence the principal posts are cut off at or just below the ground and the stumps left standing for this very purpose. This is a practice which cannot be too much encouraged. The finding of these buried " marks on the ground " will frequently end controversies, prevent law suits and avert expensive errors in construction. It is one of the duties of the surveyor to see that such landmarks are preserved as far as possible, and when it becomes necessary that they should be removed he should take such measurements and " ties " as may certainly identify their original location.

CHAPTER VII.

DEEDS WITH COMPLETE DESCRIPTIONS.

In direct contrast to deeds containing descriptions by adjoiners only is the class which, for lack of a better name, we might call " Deeds with Complete Descriptions." Such deeds usually commence with a clear location of the starting point and then continue by course and distance completely around the piece to be described with frequent reference to definite landmarks. If the deed by adjoiners, previously given in Chapter II, were to be rewritten along these lines, the description would read something like this:

" Beginning at a stake standing at the Northwest corner of the property to be conveyed at a point on the East line of the highway leading from M—— to N—— adjoining land of William Smith and running thence S $68\frac{1}{4}°$ E, 25.77 chains along land of said William Smith to land of Richard Jones as the fence now stands, thence along said Jones' land S $5\frac{1}{2}°$ E, 16.60 chains to a large Stone at the Southeast corner, thence along land now or late of John Brown S 88° W, 14.27 chains to the middle of the Spring, thence N 22° W, 57 links to a Black Oak tree, thence S $87\frac{1}{2}°$ W along said lands now or late of Brown, 11 chains to the East line of the highway, thence along the East line of said highway N $4\frac{3}{4}°$ W, 15.63 chains to the point or place of Beginning, containing within the said bounds Forty-one

Acres and 38 Square Rods of land, be the same more or less, according to a survey made by John Wolcott, County Surveyor, October 30th, 1819."

In this case the surveyor has clear and specific directions for his guidance, but actual practice will show that this is by no means an unalloyed blessing, for while these directions point the line he is to follow they are also liable to restrict him very severely. If the description were surely exact and accurate, as most modern descriptions are intended to be, the case would be different, but the descriptions of these older deeds is in general only approximate in accordance with the loose methods of conveyance of their time. How is the surveyor to tell what items are to be followed minutely, what ones are to be taken with allowance and what ones are to be thrown out altogether? In the foregoing instance it is taken for granted that there have been no clerical errors in the field notes, the description furnished by the surveyor or the deed as drawn.

In the first place the courses in the above description are given only to quarter degrees, which allows and practically necessitates an error of some minutes in the bearing of every course in the description. In the second place the original survey was probably run with an old-fashioned surveyor's compass, which is a crude instrument at best. Concerning the compass in the present case we do not know whether its meridian coincided exactly with the line of sight, whether the needle was accurately centered and moved freely on the pin or that the compass ring did not contain minute fragments of iron which might attract the needle.   Still further we have no proof that John Wolcott did not read the needle through steel-bowed spectacles.   Beside this we do not know whether he took backsights as well as foresights, whether he made allowance for diurnal variation or whether he was troubled in his work by local attraction.   Incidentally we do not know whether the same causes of local attraction exist to-day that existed in 1819 or whether the ones observable to-day were then present.

It is possible of course to determine the true meridian by observations of the Polar Star or by solar apparatus, but the exigencies of ordinary surveying frequently preclude both these methods.   Granted that the meridian can be established on the ground and that the exact declination of the needle in 1819 for the locality is known, how nearly will the line thus determined agree with the line as originally surveyed when the original record itself is so involved in probable and indeterminable error?   It seems that the old proverb, " A chain is as strong as its weakest link," is singularly applicable in the present instance.   The presence in the original fieldwork of a single one of the many possible errors makes it a very uncertain matter whether the line carefully established from meridian agrees at all closely with the old line on the ground as it was surveyed nearly a century ago.

Nor do the possibilities of error in description lie in the compass bearings alone.   There are perhaps still greater certainties of error in the chaining. We do not know certainly whether John Wolcott held his chain level or laid it along the ground. He may have struck a compromise between the two by always running full-length chains and holding them as nearly horizontal as the ground, however rugged, would allow — a method which has been done. In any case, if the country were rough, we are practically sure that the chain was considerably off the horizontal a large part of the time. In case of running parallel with a hedgerow or overgrown fence, we do not know whether he actually determined his offset points at right angles to the true stations before chaining or whether he simply laid out an equal distance at each end and " guessed " that he had established his chaining points opposite the stations. Furthermore we do not know how much the line was obstructed at the time of the original survey, how high the chain had to be held or what methods were used to determine the ground points under the ends of the chain.

Among this mass of probable errors it seems hopeless at first to think of reaching anything like definite results, but there is a mitigating circumstance which has not been mentioned. The old surveyors were more particular, it often seems, about leaving behind them permanent marks than are the surveyors of to-day. The modern surveyor is prone to run an instrument traverse where he can do so most easily, and from this he runs offsets to the corners which he marks with stakes none too large. As a result the actual line between corners is untraversed and unmarked. The old surveyors used larger corner stakes; they generally held closely to the course and frequently set line stakes at all compass stations, blazing the timber with a liberal hand.

I have in memory an old surveyor who at an advanced age took with him to the grave a knowledge of property relations which the younger men who have come after him may never hope to acquire, but whose methods of work became fixed in the days when less accuracy was demanded. His bearings were seldom closer than 5 minutes and accurate measurements would often shorten his distances ten feet in the thousand in rough and hilly country. But as a marker of a line he had few equals. If his map called for a stake in a certain place, there on the ground would be found a short strong post of locust about one foot tall. If his map called for a stone, you would find a stone that required a crow bar to move it, and his marked trees carried the scars forever. His courses and distances were inaccurate in the modern sense of the word, but they were always sure guides to the immediate vicinity of clear and substantial landmarks defining the actual boundaries.

Considering, then, all the uncertainty connected with description of land and the possible and probable errors which may exist in each case, I have been led to adopt in my own work the " Principle of Cumulative Evidence." It seems that, either rightly or wrongly, it is incumbent on the surveyor to collect all the evidence in each case and to carry his work along the lines of the preponderance of probability. In nearly all cases, while some of the data are either ambiguous or even conflicting, there is usually a large preponderance of evidence which points more or less clearly to one solution of the problem, and my own experience, containing some few examples, leads me to believe that this generally indicated solution is probably the right one. I have generally found that this line of reasoning appeals pretty strongly to all parties interested and that there is a general willingness to abide by a decision so reached. The fact that you have been willing to collect all data possible and hear all sides of the case begets confidence, and the rest is largely a matter of common sense.

If, however, the evidence for and against re-locating an old line in a certain place is pretty evenly divided, it is my belief that a conference of all parties interested should be arranged with a view to establishing a line by agreement, as a sure and safe way of preserving the peace and fixing the boundary for the years to come.

In the description mentioned at the beginning of this chapter it will be noted that most of the courses are very long, as, for instance, the first course of 25.77 chains or a little over 1700 feet. It will be readily seen that a deflection of a very few minutes at one end will cause a serious departure by the time the other end of the course is reached. Hence, if the compass is taken as the only guide of direction, the slightest error in correcting the variation will have disastrous results, supposing that the original record was perfect; and furthermore, 25.77 chains is a long distance to have been chained accurately in the old days. The deed states that this course was run " as the fence now stands." Any traces then of this old boundary are to be regarded as evidence in point, and it will be very remarkable if a number of remains are not found somewhere along the line. A bearing taken with the proper care along the general line of these landmarks should show very nearly by actual measurement how much the compass has changed since the time of the original survey. If this actual variation agrees with the theoretical variation, so much the better. The distance named in the description will enable the surveyor to tell when he approaches the near vicinity of the northeast corner, but the position of the corner should be determined from the sum total of evidence. Old stakes, fence remains, marked timber, lines along which the land has been cleared, marks of old balks or hedgerows, claims of adjoiners and testimony of old residents all have their place in the body of evidence on which the corner may be reëstablished. The dimension named in the deed should be binding only in the case of total lack of other trustworthy evidence. In nine cases our of ten the careful measurements of to-day will overrun the point where the corner originally existed.

It is not necessary, however, to settle the first course as the first step. Careful investigation may prove that matters are much clearer and much more certain in the vicinity of the stone at the southeast corner. It may be that

the line from the stone to the center of the spring is very
clear and that the variation of the compass may be best
established along this line. It is also quite possible that
the field marks indicating the back line or second course
of the description may be clear near the stone and that, by
tracing these backward, evidence previously overlooked
may be found showing where this course meets the first
course, the result being the establishment of the northeast
corner which was before more or less uncertain.

In short, no fixed rule of procedure can be laid down,
and the realization of this seems to me to be the first step
toward a right solution of problems of this nature. I do
not mean by this that the matter should be gone at hap-
hazard, but that the mind should be in a receptive condition, ready to give a hearing to all evidence and quick to
analyze, arrange and weigh this evidence. Furthermore
the mind should give its first attention to the broader
consideration of the case, coming down to details and
minutiæ later. To this end I have always found it advan-
tageous to go completely around the piece of land to be
surveyed in the company of the owner, hearing all he has
to say and noticing the main features and the landmarks
as far as possible. It is better that this should be done
several days before the actual fieldwork begins, in order
that there may be mapped out in the mind some definite
plan of work fitting the conditions in hand. A plot of the
piece of land in question, made according to the description given in the deed, will often prove very useful as a

starting point from which to work out toward a plan of common-sense procedure in making the actual survey.

Between the two extreme classes of descriptions, those with full dimensions and those with no dimensions, there are all kinds of intermediate varieties. Some deeds describe partly by adjoiners and partly by course and distance, some by linear dimensions only, and there have been some of the sides described by compass bearing only. Others are plainly made up in whole or in part from courses and distances borrowed from the descriptions of the several adjoiners, regardless of the different variations of the compass as determined by the different dates of the different component surveys.

No two of these problems are alike, but they are all open to the same method of investigation and solution, in accordance with the preponderance of evidence from all sources carefully collected, thoroughly analyzed and honestly weighed.

CHAPTER VIII.

SOURCES OF ERROR IN DESCRIPTIONS.

In the description in the previous chapter it has been taken for granted that there have been no clerical errors in recording the field notes or in transcribing them into the deed. In addition to this the actual date of the survey and the name of the surveyor are given. The former gives some definite basis on which to make compass corrections, while it is possible that something is known of the special idiosyncrasies of this particular surveyor. But it can perhaps be fairly said that in these respects this particular deed is an exception to the established order.

The descriptions to be found in many deeds are but dreary inheritances from the past. It frequently happens that circumstances require a surveyor to follow back the title of a piece of land of which he has been furnished only the description from the last transfer. He then frequently finds that the description does not apply to the time of this particular transfer at all, but has been handed down slavishly from transfer to transfer — from decade to decade. This is not necessarily the result of ignorance or penuriousness, but is frequently based on the desire to make sure that the piece of land conveyed is *exactly* the same piece that was conveyed by the next previous deed. In fact most deeds contain a clause stating that this is

" the same piece of land formerly conveyed by X—— to Z——, dated so-and-so and recorded so-and-so." Of course this all means that the date of the original survey is so very uncertain that there is no basis upon which to correct the compass, unless the search should chance to establish the time of the original survey in a fairly definite manner. It may at least be said that a few experiences of this sort remove all confidence in one's ability to make accurate compass corrections from the data contained in the ordinary deed. Indeed it is often much easier to fix the approximate date of the original survey from the actually measured compass correction of a known line in the field.

Besides this uncertainty of date there are often distinct clerical errors in transcription or even in the original field notes. When there is reason to doubt the description a careful search for what mistake would *probably* have been made under these particular circumstances will often lead to a discovery of what the proper record should have been.

It is not an uncommon matter to find that the bearing has been recorded in the wrong quadrant, especially if the bearing approaches closely due east or due west. Somewhat rarer is the error of reading the compass backward. Suppose that the bearing is N 33° W and that the surveyor is reading the end of the needle nearest him, under which circumstances the figures on the compass ring would be inverted, causing a certain possibility of confusion. His eye, instead of catching the 30 and reading on to the left, catches the 40 and reads on to the right. The result is

that he records the bearing as N 47° W instead of N 33° W
as it should be.   It would seem that these errors ought to
come out in balancing the survey at the time of the original
computation, but this is not always the case, for I have
seen a very bad quadrant error carried straight on and
plotted in the map; while in unclosed surveys, such as
those of highways, where there is no computation, there is
no way of discovering the error after it has once been made.

It is always well at the start to plot out on the paper
the description from the deed in order to find errors of
this kind, if any are present.   There was a certain description where two courses were given as northeast.   When
plotted thus, a most remarkable outline with great error
of closure was the result.   Knowing something of the locality, I felt confident that these courses should be made
southeast instead.   As soon as this change was made the
survey closed in a very satisfactory manner, and subsequent fieldwork proved my theory correct.

Far less easy to locate are errors in copying figures, yet a
logical course of procedure will frequently enable one to
make the right correction.   I remember one case where
the description was supposed to follow the remains of an
old worm fence and the actual survey agreed with this
description in a most satisfactory manner.   Suddenly, on
a course given as S 7° E, the line deflected several feet
from the fence and on the following courses continued
parallel to it.   It seemed that the surveyor might have
read the compass backward and recorded 7° when he

meant 3°. This correction improved the trouble but did not entirely do away with it. I then took the actual bearing of the fence, corrected it and found that the original bearing must have been 4° instead of 7°. The explanation was simple. Someone in writing the 4 had made the first downstroke very short, had made the cross-stroke very high and had carried it only until it met the long downstroke. Someone making a later copy of this description had mistaken the distorted 4 for an elaborate 7 and had copied it as such.

When such clerical errors occur on maps they can frequently be discovered by going over the map with scale and protractor, the actual lines of the map being correct while the accompanying legend is not. Other errors again can only be corrected from the actual conditions as found in the field. For some errors no logical explanation can be found. They must be corrected according to the best dictates of common sense.

Before leaving the subject of deeds attention should be called to one further point of interest, that for purposes of getting back to an original boundary or settling a dispute, several deeds, though equally explicit, are not necessarily of equal value. This is especially true with reference to the determination of boundaries along highways. Most highways are described in the public records by a survey, the courses, distances and width of the road being clearly given. Theoretically the descriptions of properties adjoining such a road should come to the recorded boundaries

of the road and no farther. It is a fact, however, that
these boundaries along roads are the most unstable of all
boundaries for the simple reason that, while each man
watches his neighbor to see that there is no transgression
of the line between them, all parties concerned are apt to
combine to borrow as much land from the public highway
as possible. As a rule a highway record is rather difficult
to reëstablish, and in cases of small places and house lots
the ordinary deed, outside of city limits, makes no pre-
tense of defining the road in accordance with its official
boundaries. The survey has usually been made at small
charges by some local surveyor, the object being simply to
" get something we can put in the deed."

As a result some deeds bordering along such a road,
notably those of a date nearest to that at which the road
itself was put on record, may be very valuable not only
with reference to the piece of property which they describe but also in connection with determining the actual
location of the road itself. They more probably represent the conditions before there was any encroachment on
the highway, while the deeds of other pieces of land on
the same street, though they may agree exactly with the
present lines of possession, may be based upon surveys
made after the fences had been pushed out on to land
properly belonging to the public. There is a case where
two small streets together formed a T-shaped court, one
street forming the upright of the T and the other the
crossbar at the top. Both had been recorded something

like fifty years ago, but the official boundaries had been very much neglected. It became necessary to define the boundaries of these streets, since it was generally believed that there had been wholesale encroachment on the highway. A careful examination of the road record, and of the deeds which were made at about the same time and which also referred specifically to these streets as new streets, gave sufficient data for locating the limits of the road successfully. There were other deeds, however, where the case was very different. There was one in particular of a property located at the corner where the two streets met. In this deed the description agreed almost exactly with the land as found in possession, but these lines of possession at one corner encroached several feet on the highway. Investigation showed that for nearly ten years after the recording of the street this corner land had lain unfenced and had practically been regarded as common land. When finally a fence was erected it was placed without reference to the street lines which had been lost sight of meanwhile. The survey for the deed was probably made as the fence stood, and thus it came to pass that a description which agreed with long-established lines of possession was finally found to be utterly at variance with the road record.

From the above it will readily be seen that it is a delicate matter, in the case of determining a boundary controversy, to sort out the valuable deeds from those which are worthless from the surveyor's standpoint. It requires not only good judgment but a considerable amount of tact as well, for it is a trying matter to convince one party in the altercation that his deed is worthless as evidence while his opponent's is of value. The surveyor is pretty sure to incur criticism in any case.

Of course a large part of the foregoing does not apply to sections where property lines and especially street lines are marked by accurately set stone monuments. In such cases the boundaries are already settled. The suggestions are intended to apply to old acreage and long-settled country communities where the loosely established boundaries of long ago have seldom been verified, and where, during the lapse of easy-going years, the landmarks have been lost or forgotten. It is such lines and such landmarks that it is difficult to reëstablish when the requirements of the present day demand them.

CHAPTER IX.

THE RELATIONS OF THE SURVEYOR AND THE LAWYER.

BEFORE leaving this general subject it would perhaps be well to consider for a few moments the relation between the surveyor and the one who may perhaps be called his co-worker — the lawyer.

Surveys are usually made in order to furnish the descriptions to be used in legal instruments and the data necessary for legal proceedings. The surveyor does not necessarily look upon a survey in the same light as does the man of law, and he must be governed largely by the particular legal requirements of the case in hand. While the surveyor naturally looks for the intention implied in the earliest conveyance of a piece of land and seeks to get back to the original boundaries, the lawyer may sweep aside all this exact and careful work and require a survey according to the boundaries of to-day, on the ground of undisputed possession for a number of years. Yet the lawyer will promptly admit that the course followed by the surveyor was the proper course for the *surveyor*, the responsibility of departing from the ancient record resting entirely with himself. Furthermore the lawyer is generally very glad to know what the original conditions actually were, no matter how far he may subsequently depart from them.

I have said that the surveyor must be largely governed by the legal requirements of the case in hand, but I do not mean by this that he should endeavor to make legal decisions for himself. The surveyor is usually employed by a lawyer direct or by a man who has an attorney looking after his interests, and the survey is usually wanted for some special and particular purpose. Though the surveyor may not at all approve the lines he is directed to follow, I do not think that he can very well refuse to do the work unless it is very clear that he is making himself a party to questionable proceedings. In case he does not fully agree with the instructions which he receives I think that he should make his employer or his employer's attorney shoulder completely the responsibility for those instructions, and that he should retain written evidence of the same if possible. If a moral issue is at stake he should refuse the work rather than enter upon an undertaking which he believes to be questionable.

I think there is no doubt that the legal intricacies connected with the search and guaranteeing of complicated titles are beyond the province and the full appreciation of the ordinary surveyor, yet he must render intelligent help to the lawyer who is attending to the same. I think that in these cases he should obtain the most explicit directions concerning the measurements which he is to make and that he should make a most full and careful report to the lawyer of the conditions as found on the ground, and that he should then ask for full directions as to what the final survey must show and should assume responsibility for absolutely nothing but the honesty and accuracy of his work. By so doing he will be certain of keeping his own hands clean and of retaining the respect of all those by whom he is employed.

It is a curious fact that a great many lawyers who are continually dealing with land transfers are grossly ignorant of the simplest details of surveying — I should say that the minority know the number of feet in a chain. As a result many useful details which the surveyor would gladly furnish in connection with the piece of land in question are to many of them difficult of comprehension or absolutely meaningless. On the other hand the surveyor is probably equally ignorant of the law of property. A frank recognition by each of his own limitation is, I think, the first step to a sound understanding and furnishes a starting point from which both may work together toward accurate and satisfactory results.

CHAPTER X.

HOUSE LOTS.

WHILE it may be said that in general the most important problems that vex the surveyor arise in connection with acreage and the determination of old boundaries, yet there is a class of smaller surveys which, in its way, is capable of giving infinite trouble. This is the group of house-lot surveys. In fact I think it may be fairly said that there is more strife and litigation over the boundaries of these small holdings than there is over the boundaries of large tracts.

The reasons for this are not difficult to find. Usually land which is divided into lots is held at a much higher valuation than that which lies in large tracts, and an inch error one way or the other is a very much more serious matter. Moreover since the dimensions are comparatively small and extremely specific, property owners feel that the surveyor should be able to show them *exactly* where their boundaries lie. This expectation is thoroughly reasonable in case of modern lot layouts in large communities where property limits are minutely defined, but such surveys usually come under the hands of city engineers and seldom fall to the lot of those whose work lies in country-towns and villages or at best in the suburbs of lesser cities.

It seldom happens that an engineer opening an office in such a community will be called upon at first to cut up a piece of property into building lots, but it is highly probable that one of his earliest orders will be to set the corner stakes of a plot according to a map of lots already in existence. He may perhaps be materially aided in this work by a few suggestions as to the methods in which country property has usually been subdivided. Subdivided properties in the country are usually of two kinds:

1. Properties controlled by Real Estate Companies.

These properties are usually independent units. They are bought and handled purely as money-making enterprises and they are laid out entirely with a view to bringing in the greatest possible returns on the investment. As a result they usually bear no relation whatever to the adjoining properties. They usually have a complete street system of their own which is entirely independent of the road system of the town, except that it connects with one or more highways already existing. Long experience in handling land in the market has given these real estate companies the knowledge of how to cut up the land most profitably, and they generally furnish the surveyor a plan of subdivision which he is expected to follow within the limits of common sense. For this plan they require a careful map of the boundaries of the property showing its relation to the adjoining highways and also the location of all buildings standing upon it. If the map also shows clearly the boundaries between woodland and cleared land

and the location of all streams, ponds, swamps, ravines, etc., in short any points of knowledge which may be useful in subdividing the property, so much the better. Guided by this map the owners will make a plan for subdivision which it will be the surveyor's later work to actually place upon the grounds.

2. Properties owned by Private Individuals usually not Professional Real Estate Men.

It sometimes happens that Mr. Smith, looking over his more or less extensive property, finds a portion which is at present yielding small returns, and it strikes him that it would be an excellent idea to cut it up into building lots and sell it to small holders. Feeling fairly well convinced that the town is going to grow in that direction he proceeds to carry his plan into effect.

The actual work of subdividing the land is carried out with all degrees of wisdom and unwisdom. I have seen an owner lay out lots with a common fifty-foot " metallic " tape, using no transit and making no map. As the prices which he asked for his lots were singularly fair he made many sales; and in all cases he made the conveyances and prepared the deeds personally. I have known of another case where the lines were run, not with a transit but with a plain surveyor's compass, many of the main lines being of such a nature that it was impossible to see from one end to the other. The chain or tape work was such as might be expected from a man who would lay out building lots by a magnetic needle. A map was then prepared according to what this survey was *intended* to be and the deeds were drawn by a third party who knew very little about the conditions in the case. These instances are of course extreme and the final complications arising in each of these properties may easily be imagined.

The conditions under which country property is subdivided are usually somewhat as follows:

A man — the Mr. Smith above mentioned — owns a piece of property bounded on one side by a highway and he decides to cut up this property into lots. If it is a small property he opens one street through the middle of it from the highway to the back boundary; if it is fairly large he opens two or more parallel streets. These streets are usually at right angles to the highway and are spaced a number of lot widths apart, often without any particular attention being paid to the fitness of the land for road building. All lots that can be so arranged are made to face on the public highway. The remainder are made to face, as far as possible, on the main streets which have been cut through and the balance are faced on cross streets placed at suitable (or unsuitable) intervals at right angles to the main streets. These cross streets run to the side lines of the property and stop.

Inasmuch as the exact boundary of the public highway is seldom known, and as its course frequently changes one or more times in passing across the front of the property, it is seldom attempted to make the highway the starting point of the lot layout. The intersection of the first cross street with the main street or streets is usually made the place of beginning, and from this point the property is cut up into blocks which shall, as far as possible, contain an exact number of rectangular lots of the dimensions which have been decided upon by the owners. It will be seen, however, that all those lots which touch the outer boundaries of the property will, in all probability, have irregular shapes and dimensions, determined by the direction of these boundaries at the different points of contact. Such lots are the " remainders " resulting from this sum in division and for convenience may be spoken of as " residual lots " or simply as " residuals."

It only remains now to make a map of the property with an ornate title and imposing names for the streets. This map will show all lots by number, the position of the streets and also the exact dimensions of all the *standard* lots. The dimensions of the " residuals," if given at all, are followed by the " plus-and-minus " sign or are preceded by the abbreviation " abt." to show that these dimensions which come in contact with the claims of other adjoiners are not guaranteed. The same reservation is usually employed in giving the depths of the lots which face on the public highway, while the oblique frontages caused by the change of direction of the side line of the highway are frequently left entirely blank. Of course there are lot maps where all these dimensions have been carefully worked out and where the description of each lot is complete and accurate, but the above has, I think, been the more common practice in lot maps of the kind described.

It may be that Mr. Jones, one of the adjoiners of the property described above, having seen how successful Mr. Smith was in his enterprise, may decide to do the same thing and cut up his property into lots, and the probabilities are that he will follow the same general plan. If his land is in the rear of Mr. Smith's he will continue the main street through his own property and will make cross streets in much the same manner as did Mr. S. If his land lies at one side he will cut main streets from the highway, parallel with Mr. Smith's, and will continue that gentleman's cross streets at least to the nearest main street.

This seems a very simple process, but in reality there are certain complications which frequently arise. Mr. Jones, in having the survey made for the map, will direct the surveyor to follow the description given in his own deed and frequently (especially if the deeds are old) this description will not agree in all details with the description according to which Mr. Smith laid out his map. If the same surveyor does the work in both cases he will, or should, use his best endeavors to prevent any complications, but in case the second map is made by a person who is unfamiliar with the details of the first layout, in all probability there will be some point where the lots of one map will overlap those of the other or else there will be a gap left between. I do not think that this trouble can be always rightly charged against the surveyor, for the reason that if he were to do sufficient work to safeguard against all possibilities of complications in any of the adjoining properties which might at some future day be cut up into lots, he would have the pleasure of doing a large amount of work at his own expense. In all probability Mr. Jones would flatly decline to pay for anything but the work done in actually cutting up his land and in determining its boundaries with a fair degree of accuracy according to the description contained in his own deed. I think on the whole that a surveyor has done his duty when he has made all reasonable endeavor to prevent misunderstanding, and has made clear on his map what dimensions are to be considered as not absolutely certain. If the person who draws the deeds is equally careful, there can be little danger of serious controversy. Half the strife concerning the boundaries of residual lots arises from the omission of the qualifying terms which should be used concerning these doubtful dimensions, and which have been clearly shown, or should have been clearly shown, by the surveyor in the map on which the deeds were based.

CHAPTER XI.

HOUSE LOTS (concluded).

ANOTHER complication which sometimes arises is in the matter of extending the streets from one property to another. An illustration may be in point. There once came into my hands a map of lots laid out as follows: A main street ran through the middle of the property with a cross street at right angles to it. At the extreme edge of the property lay a street, which we will call " Edge Street," distant 400 feet from the cross street and parallel with it. Edge Street had been formed from a residual strip 30 feet wide given by the property in question and a strip 20 feet wide given by the adjoining property. Four hundred feet from the cross street I found the old surveyor's stake marking the intersection of Edge Street with the main street before mentioned, and I set the street monument accordingly. At this stage a lot owner on the main street made a protest and produced deeds showing that instead of 400 feet the distance between the cross street and Edge Street was really 405 feet. A search in the County Clerk's office showed that there was on file there a map of the property in which, previous to filing, certain dimensions had been erased and altered. One of the lots had been broadened from 50 feet to 55 feet and the strip thrown into Edge Street had been narrowed from 30 feet to 25 feet. In accordance with the recorded map I moved the monument 5 feet, thus increasing the distance between streets from 400 to 405 feet. It will be seen that there still existed a discrepancy of 5 feet between the corner as the original surveyor left it staked in the field and the corner as shown on the map filed with the County Clerk. In other words, the stakes in the field had never been moved to fit the revised map placed on file. Under ordinary circumstances the final establishment of the corner should have settled all trouble, but it had happened that already the owner of the adjoining property had cut it up into lots and had extended Edge Street through the entire length of it. Unfortunately the surveyor had extended this street from the stakes existing in the field, having no possible way of knowing that they did not agree with the map filed at the County Seat. This extension of Edge Street was opened, lots were sold along it, trees were planted and houses built. The result of the discovery of the error of location of the first part of Edge Street and its correction by moving the whole alignment 5 feet can readily be seen. In the first property this shifting was easily effected since this part of Edge Street had never been improved, but the permanent improvements of Edge Street in the adjoining property made such a " moving over " impossible. As a result, at the boundary line between the two properties the street " broke joints " to the amount of 5 feet, and when this private street later became a public highway the matter had to be adjusted by inserting a small oblique course to join these two unmatched portions.

It quite frequently happens that where the ground is uneven, careful measurements will show that there is not sufficient land between clearly established streets to meet the demands of the map or of the deeds which have already been filed. Sometimes, rarely, in auction sales of lots, glaring errors will exist in dimensions. I remember one property where such errors occurred as the following,

Sales dimension, 420 feet, actual dimension, 412.1 feet;

Sales dimension, 335 feet, actual dimension, 355.5 feet;

Sales dimension, 150 feet, actual dimension, 130.75 feet; with others of the same nature. Unfortunately in the haste of the sale these lots were all sold by specified dimensions without a single qualifying word. It can readily be seen that the final adjustment was more profitable to the surveyor than to the parties of the first and second parts.

How can a surveyor bring order out of such chaos as this? How can he adjust all the discrepancies in the work of those who have gone before him? The answer is simple — he cannot. But he can do a great deal toward mitigating conditions. He must be able to gather all information bearing on the problems and weigh it accurately, he must be able to interpret a deed to a nicety and to determine unerringly the priority of conflicting claims, he must be willing to bring about friendly relations and mutual concessions between adjoiners and he can advise his clients against accepting unsatisfactory deeds. Beyond all else he must be ready to go over with endless patience innumerable repetitions of detail with interested parties who are frequently of willing mind but of slow comprehension. In short he must do all his work in such a thorough and painstaking manner that any one coming after him may find nothing to add to it.

Of one thing, however, I am firmly convinced, that it is useless for a surveyor to go into a strange subdivided property and locate any one lot with quickness, ease and accuracy. I have seen the attempt fail too many times. If one could be certain that the first layout was absolutely accurate and that the stakes had never been displaced it would be a different matter; but such is not the case. Errors of inches and sometimes of feet often occur; right angles seldom measure exactly 90 degrees and stakes are frequently moved out of line by people stumbling over them. If the surveyor would rest with an easy mind he must check up a sufficient number of streets, blocks and lots, to be sure that he has located his special lot in strict accordance with the boundaries of the streets and the claims of other landholders. To do this he will frequently have to put in many hours of work from which he must expect no immediate returns. But the fact that he has taken pains to locate the lots accurately, that he has worked out the details of the property and that he (and very likely he only) knows where the lines truly run, practically insures that all or nearly all of the future work in that property

will eventually come to him for execution. It is simply
another illustration of the fact that honesty is the best
policy.

There is one other form of the lot problem which should
be mentioned. In earlier times it was a frequent occurrence for a land owner to sell a succession of house lots
from his property. These small holdings adjoined each
other and were of all shapes and sizes, with very uncertain
relations to the highway which they bordered. Happily
they were usually fenced at an early date, and the evi-
dences of early possession are of vastly greater value than
the deed dimensions. Front and rear dimensions are usually fairly accurate, but a common line between two neigh-
bors will often have quite dissimilar lengths in the two
deeds. This is due largely to the uncertain condition of
the highway line. As stated, the lines of old possession are
very important, but in deciding a boundary controversy
it is never safe to assume that any one line of possession
is sufficiently correct to be taken as a starting point for
measurements. A sufficient number of deeds must be
examined and a sufficient number of lots checked up to
make certain of the accuracy of the possession line in
question. It may then be used as a point of departure.

To illustrate, a certain street corner which was in dispute
was recorded as being located " 25 links west of lot belonging to William Smith." The width of the Smith lot was
measured and found to be exactly 50 feet — a standard
size. Then the street corner was made 25 links beyond.

To leave no chance of error the deed of the Smith lot was procured, and it was found that the front dimension was not 50 feet but " 74 links of chain " or 48.84 feet. This led to a checking up of all other properties necessary, with the result that all lines of possession were found to be essentially correct except a part of the west fence of the Smith lot which was comparatively new. After this had been established it was easy to locate the street corner accurately and satisfactorily.

It will readily be seen that there are no fixed rules which can be laid down for the accurate handling of old lot layouts. Satisfactory results can be obtained only through care, patience and common sense and, above all, honesty.

So much for the interpretation of old lot layouts; now a word with reference to the construction of new ones. With reference to general plan there is little to say, for the reason that the owner of the land has usually some pretty clear idea of just exactly what he desires — he simply wants the surveyor to carry out his design. In cases where there is no such preconceived plan one or two suggestions may not be out of place.

1. Roads and streets should be located, as far as possible, with a view to economy in construction and maintenance, while every effort should be made to so place the streets that after grading they shall be reasonably accessible from the lots bordering them.

2. If the land is to be cut up into standard lots there is

very little room for independence of action, but if it is to be divided into somewhat variable plots much can be done in the way of locating them with reference to picturesqueness and accessibility. One further point might be made. Nearly every property has some undesirable land scattered about in one or more places. It is a mistake to make any one plot consist of undesirable land only, since it must be sold at a greatly reduced price if at all. If, however, you so divide the property that this undesirable land shall be shared in small quantities by a number of plots otherwise wholly desirable, the difficulty has been overcome. A purchaser naturally expects that he will get a little inferior land with the good and, if he gets a good house site and lawn, he is perfectly willing to take a little less satisfactory land on some other part of his plot. In other words, the idea is not to cut the land into extra fine plots and poor plots, but to so divide it that each and every plot shall have sufficient points of excellence to thoroughly compensate for the less desirable features which must be distributed in general to all purchasers. Briefly put, the plots must all be salable.

3. It is not good practice to subdivide land in the office. If the original traverse of the property has been exceptionally accurate this may be done with a fair degree of safety; but it so frequently happens that one error offsets another, that a fine balance of an entire traverse is no guarantee that the work is as perfect in all its details as this balance would seem to show. It is my belief that all streets should

be actually laid on the ground and their intersections with the boundaries of the property actually determined in the field. All complete blocks and all residual blocks should also be measured before any attempt is made to give even the approximate dimensions of residual lots. This method, while more laborious than others, is sure to give good results, and will avoid the annoying discrepancies which are so frequently found in properties divided by methods of computation only.

CHAPTER XII.

HIGHWAY RECORDS.

EXCEPT perhaps the study of the evolution of the private ownership of land, there is nothing more attractive in the realm of surveying than the evolution of the Highway or Public Road. Nor need this statement be confined to the subject in its broadest sense — the study of road building from its earliest times to the present; it is equally interesting to study the evolution of the road system of a town as set forth in the complete Town Records.

In general, history of the roads of an old district is simple. Early records made soon after the settlement simply state that a road was established from such a place to such a place. There is no attempt at description by course and distance and seldom by landmarks or adjoiners, though the width of the road is frequently given. Later follows the description by landmarks or by a statement of the properties which the road touched in its course; later still, the distance in rods from point to point appears. Subsequently come the descriptions by bearings to degrees or quarter degrees and distances in chains and links, and it is in this form that the Road Records of most rural highways, as far as I have been able to observe, actually exist. At the time in their history when surveys were made to this particular degree of accuracy the roads were already so well established that they required no subsequent change, and their records have continued to exist in this form. Later roads are more minutely described, but they are seldom the main roads of a community.

Recent roads, as just stated, are usually fully described in the public records, and in further explanation maps are placed on file. Furthermore the actual location of such road lines on the ground is usually clearly marked by stone monuments accurately set. Such roads present few serious problems to the surveyor, but when he is called upon to re-locate from the public records the actual lines of old roads inaccurately surveyed and ambiguously, if quaintly, recorded, — roads where greedy possession has encroached amazingly upon the public easement, where time and man have joined forces to obliterate the ancient landmarks, — his problem is of an entirely different kind.

Roads are all supposed to have a certain legal status which is commonly known as a " public easement." Theoretically the road is still the private property of the parties who adjoin it, with the understanding that they have loaned it to the town for use as a highway for so long as the town shall need it. Such roads are said to be " released " to the town and certain legal steps are necessary in order to make the release binding. It not infrequently happens that through carelessness or ignorance these legal steps have not been properly taken and, in case of litigation between the town and the adjoiners to the road, much annoyance arises therefrom. Some roads are actually deeded to the town and become thereby the town's actual property, but in the country, at least, these are rare. Old records also sometimes describe certain roads as " regulated " by the highway commissioners. This appears to have been a somewhat irregular and arbitrary process, a " regulated " road continuing as such on the record unless somebody with a grievance brought the law to bear upon it.

With the legal phase of these various forms of record the surveyor has little concern. He must see that his work has been in accordance with the record and that he has found the whole of that record; its legality is the concern of the town's legal adviser. I have said that it is important that the surveyor should find the *whole* of the record and this perhaps needs a word of explanation. If a road were surveyed and recorded once for all the matter of locating it on the ground would become sufficiently difficult after the lapse of years, but it frequently happens that the record is fragmentary and the fragments are hard to identify in the mass of public records.

The normal history of a main country road is usually somewhat as follows, especially if it is a rather lengthy one joining two or more villages. In the early days of a community public convenience and topographical conditions determine travel along a certain route which, in the expiration of time, is recognized as a public thoroughfare, although it may not appear at all on the public records or perhaps only in the most general terms. Later, as the community becomes more thickly settled and the value of property increases, there is a public demand that the legal status of the road shall be defined and its boundaries officially established. This forms the first *definite* record and it is a fortunate matter if the first record remains also the last. It frequently happens, however, that later in the public records you may find a petition to have a portion of this road altered. There are many reasons for doing this. It may be that the parties adjoining the road on both sides may for some cause desire it. It may be that the road requires straightening or that a slight change in the location of some portion will materially reduce the public expense of maintenance. At any rate the alteration is made and it is hardly ever known of a case where such occurrence of alteration has been noted on the *original* record. It also frequently happens that the road is altered under an entirely different name from that which it bore in the original description, and that, at the present day, the road is known by an entirely different name from either.

For instance there is a highway which at the present day is almost invariably called the Sandis Hill Road, but which was originally recorded in 1827 under the somewhat laborious title of " Highway leading from Silas Marner's Barn running southerly till it intersects the highway leading from Townsend Jackson's to Cold Spring." In 1832 it was altered under the title of " Pitkin Hollow Highway." The identity of the two roads can be discovered only by one who has an extensive knowledge of the names of the long dead adjoiners, this knowledge being aided by an incidental record reference to an intersection with a third old road the name of which has also changed. The searcher's attention having been arrested by these items of description, his conclusions are confirmed by finding a careful entry, under the alteration, of the date and page of the original description. Following is a copy of the record of the alteration in full, as it is an excellent example of the wording of an old highway record and because it furnishes several excellent illustrations of the difficulties which beset the surveyor who actually attempts to locate the bounds of such a highway.

" We the Commissioners of highways of the Town of Oysterbay in the County of Queens having in persuance of the Statute entitled ' An Act regulating highways and bridges in the Counties of Suffolk, Queens and Kings ' passed February 23rd 1830 taken a view of the highway in the said Town of Oysterbay leading from Pitkin hollow to the dwelling house of Horton Worman and finding said highway to require alteration in some parts thereof as the same was regulated and established by the Commissioners of highways of the said Town of Oysterbay on the 6th day of March 1827 and recorded in the book of the Records of highways of the said Town of Oysterbay pages 183, 184 and 185, Do hereby order and direct that the said highway be so far altered as that the center or middle line thereof shall run as follows to Wit . . . Beginning 31 Links Eastward from a Walnut tree on the West on Cæsar Brown's Land, and running from thence S 5¾° W 2.35 Chs a poplar tree making the East Line thence S 14° E 1.81 Chs— thence S 35° E 5.44 Chs — thence S 33¼° E 2.47 Chs — thence S 3° E 4.59 Chs thence S 4½° E 7.15 Chs — Thence S ½° E 2.59 Chs an apple tree on the West Line — thence S 12¼° E 2.20 Chs a white oak tree one foot East of the East Line and a walnut tree one foot West of the West Line — thence S 33½° E 1.24 Chs a wild cherry tree on the West Line — thence S 44° E 1.08 Chs, thence S 39° E 2.72 Chs an apple tree on the West Line — thence S 28° E 2.88 Chs — thence S 16° E 4.74 Chs a white oak tree on the W — thence S 12¼° E 3.19 Chs — thence S 1¾° E 1.92 Chs a walnut tree on the West Line — thence S 16¼° E till it strikes the road leading from Robert Calwell's to Horton Worman's — And that the outlines or extreme boundaries of the said highway shall be one and a half rods on each side thereof, so that the said highway shall be three rods wide throughout . . . And we do further order and direct that the Clerk of the said Town of Oysterbay forthwith post a copy of this order on the door of the house where the Annual Town meeting in said Town was last held . . . Given under our hands at the Town of Oysterbay the 28th day of July 1832.

THOMAS COCK⎫
Copy posted Aug. 6th, 1832   ISAAC WEEDS ⎬ Com rs
Chs. H. Peters   JACOB CROCKER⎭
T. Clerk."

Taken as old records go the above is a very satisfactory one for the reason that a large number of landmarks are specified. But it will be noticed that many points essential for the exact location of the road upon the ground are entirely lacking. For instance the distance of the starting point from the walnut tree is given but the exact bearing is omitted, the general term " eastward " being used instead. Also there is not the remotest attempt to define the point on the *original survey* where the alteration begins or where it ends, so that it is impossible to determine to what courses the alterations apply. There is no way of telling at what points on the side lines of the respective courses the various landmarks stand — we only know that a certain tree stood *somewhere* on the side line of a certain course. Finally, Who was Cæsar Brown and where did he live? As a matter of fact several people were asked, but they had never heard the name. Finally I went to one of the oldest men in town and asked him about it. " Yes," said he, " I remember Cæsar Brown when I was a boy. He was an old man and that he lived about where A——'s land is. If you go there I think you will find the hole where the cellar of his house used to be." On visiting the place the cellar hole was easily found and, what was more, the walnut tree, though dead, was still standing.

I have digressed a good deal from the main line of thought, but I think that the above details will make two points clear: first, that it is very difficult to find sufficiently clear data for re-locating an old road with even approximate accuracy and, secondly, that it is of the utmost importance to obtain the complete record of the road including all changes which it may have undergone.

The genesis of all highways is not the same. While many come from the legalizing of certain ancient traveled ways, others are of gradual growth. Under the general discussion of lot layouts it has been shown how in the process of developing real estate a street may have successive stages of extension as it is carried from one property on into another. In the old days this process of development was so gradual that some years might intervene between the successive steps of street extension. On this account it frequently happened that the street did not go onto the records as a whole, but piece by piece, each section frequently being described by the land through which it was laid out and the final accepted name of the street never appearing at all. For instance we will say that a street now known as Summit Street runs through the lands of Smith, Jones and Brown. Smith opened the portion through his land first and it was described on the records as " Road through James Smith's Land." Five years later Jones decided to extend it through his property and it was duly recorded as " Highway through William Jones' Land." Finally Brown carried it through his land to the highway adjoining him, naming it " Summit Street." It would then very likely be recorded as " Summit Street through John Brown's Land to the Turnpike." To get a complete record of Summit Street all three records must be looked up and fitted together.

CHAPTER XIII.

RE-RUNNING OLD HIGHWAY RECORDS.

THE actual process of "running out" an old road record is even more difficult in practice than it is in theory. No actual rules can be given, but some general suggestions may be helpful. It will readily be seen that in the case of a road several miles in length, even though the starting point can be exactly found, an error of one minute in the direction of the first course will produce an enormous departure at the end of the run. When one also takes into consideration that the original survey was probably run with a compass and that no attempt was made in most cases to read more closely than quarter degrees, it will be seen that all hope of exact re-location by instrumental methods only must be abandoned at once.

If the surveyor has been so fortunate as to be able to locate the starting point and compute the variation of the compass, what is the next step after running and marking the first course? Shall the succeeding courses be run by the needle or shall they be located by turning off deflection angles? Theoretically it seems to me that the former is the better method, since by it one may probably put oneself more nearly under the conditions under which the original surveyor worked. In actual practice it has been found that better results have been obtained by turning off the deflection angles. Let the second course, then, be turned off and run according to the record and the end of it marked. The succeeding courses are to be run in the same manner until the next landmark is reached, unless there is good reason to believe that the work is going seriously wrong. It is very seldom, however, that the newly surveyed line is found to have exactly the same relations to the landmarks that the record demands. If the error of direction is large perhaps the simplest way is to make some effort to approximate the angular correction necessary, after which the courses may be re-run. It should be borne in mind that during all this process most careful account should be taken of all things that may help to throw light on the problem. Marks on trees along the sides of the road, the position of ancient lines of possession, the testimony of adjoiners and the descriptions contained in their deeds are all possible valuable sources of information which must not be slighted.

It sometimes happens that both ends of some important course are described with such detail with reference to their direction and distance from the corners of buildings still standing that it is possible to locate this course immediately. When this condition exists the first running of the courses will probably approximate closely to the original line of survey. Yet even in this case the final location of the line must in all probability be based on common-sense conclusions drawn from a study of all the evidence obtainable.

The surveyor will be aided in reaching these conclusions by remembering the three following generalities which are well substantiated by fact.

1. That the original record, while an invaluable general guide, is only approximately accurate.

2. That in old roads the record was originally made in accordance with the main lines of possession then existing, and that such lines of possession as were at variance with the newly recorded road were probably moved into their proper position at an early date.

3. That the stations of the original survey — the points where the course changed — were very frequently exactly at those points where the road was intersected by the cross fences between adjoining properties.

The previous suggestions apply more especially to finding the *approximate* position of the line of the old record. When this approximate position has been found — a position for the line where it agrees fairly well with the record and the sum total of the evidence obtainable. The following method has been found to be excellent for getting it into its final and most nearly accurate location. Mark each station with a stake if possible — if not, with a spike well driven down — and take sufficient ties to every station so that its exact location can be found again without fail. Make an accurate traverse of the courses thus marked and determine carefully the direction and distance from the most convenient stations to every landmark which can be identified and to every point whose position must be

known. These notes should then be plotted in the office
on a large sheet of paper on which should also be drawn
two rectangular axes — one running north and south and
one east and west — conveniently placed. Next every co-
ordinate point in the survey with reference to these axes
should be computed and properly noted on the drawing.
The next thing is to determine by careful study how far
and in what direction the surveyed line must be moved in
order to bring it as nearly as possible into the same relation
with the landmarks as that shown by the record. Valuable
suggestions are often obtained by plotting both the new
survey and the old record on separate pieces of tracing
paper and superimposing them.

Having determined upon the amount which the new line
must be moved in order to bring it into its proper relation
to the landmarks, compute new coördinates for each of its
stations in the new position. It is then a simple matter to
compute the direction and distance for each station from
the stake left in the road to the point which the station
must finally occupy. It should be noted that the principle of coördinates is of universal application. By far
the greater part of the old road records describe the survey
of the center line and the distance from the center line of
the side lines. The coördinates of these center-line stations, either approximate or real, being known, it is manifestly easy to compute the distance and direction to any
point on the outer boundaries of the road and also to determine the relation of any point on these lines to any

building or obstruction, the position of which is in question. Familiarity with this method of computation cannot be too strenuously urged.

While the great majority of country-road records give the description by the center line, there are a few which describe one of the side lines instead.   These are most easily handled by computing from the record of the side line what the center line would be and then running out this center line.   You undoubtedly will find that in all cases it is thoroughly profitable to plot the old record with all its landmarks on paper before going into the field.   It frequently happens that past masters of highways were not past masters of the English language, and many old records are exceedingly complicated and confused in their wording. If the interpretation is carefully worked out step by step and transferred to paper in actual lines and points the meaning usually becomes perfectly clear.   A blueprint of this drawing is a most useful thing when it comes to the actual outdoor work.

It sometimes happens that in searching the records for the description of a particular road it is difficult to identify that record when found.   If, then, the record believed to be the correct one be plotted on paper and the resulting map be compared with the map of the desired road as shown on the State Atlas Sheets or some other reliable chart, it is usually very easy to decide whether further search is necessary.

CHAPTER XIV.

LAYING OUT NEW ROADS.

It would not be right to leave the general subject of roads without a few words of suggestion in the matter of laying out and recording new highways. If the surveyor comes in touch at all with the local government of his town his first work will very probably be to lay out a new road, or, more probably, to make a survey of a private road already existing in order that it may be placed upon the records of the town and made a public highway. The common methods of procedure in such cases is for a number of property owners along a road to petition the town to put the road on the highway list. If the petition is accepted all persons owning land affected are called upon to " sign a release," by which they agree to release the town from all liability for any injury which may come to their property through the opening of this road. The next thing is to survey and mark the road in order that a description of it may be put upon record and a description incorporated in the release. The surveyor is expected to make this survey and to prepare the map and description.

From my own experience I am of the belief that the determination of the exact boundary of such a private road is a rather delicate affair. Among the petitioners there are pretty sure to be one or more who are not very enthu-siastic in the matter and who are very jealous of their rights. Of course all principles of engineering require that a road should consist of straight lines and satisfactory curves, all laid with reference to ease of construction and economy of maintenance. The prejudices and jealousies of adjoiners, however, frequently make such a plan hopeless of execution, and it is possible to place the road only in that location where they are willing to have it go. The first and most important thing is to determine accurately where each owner's private boundary along the road is located. Some owners will be willing to make concessions to the common good, while some will not yield an inch. All that the surveyor can do is to keep on hand an inexhaust-ible supply of patience and good nature and to do the best he can with the conditions as he finds them.

The survey of the road having been made, the boundaries should be marked after the method commonly employed by the town, though stone monuments should be used if possible. Since stakes and even monuments are sometimes buried and at times actually dug up, it is very desirable that there should be some additional means of locating the lines of the road easily and accurately. Accordingly all im-portant points on the survey should have their location clearly defined with reference to plain and permanent land-marks wherever this is possible, and these " ties " should be shown on the map, though for the sake of clearness they may sometimes be wisely omitted from the written record.

The description prepared for entry should be constructed with great care. It should convey the intended meaning without a shadow of ambiguity, and it should, in no particular, mean either more or less than it was intended to mean. It is perhaps well to go over the first draft of such a description with the town's legal adviser before offering it for record, in order that no loophole may be left for future litigation.

CHAPTER XV.

RESPONSIBILITIES OF THE SURVEYOR.

THIS completes the suggestions which I wished to offer, but I would like in conclusion to say a few words in a general manner. This very brief treatise is not intended as a handbook for surveyors in any way; it is not didactic — it is suggestive only. It is intended to give a little light to men thrown, for perhaps the first time, on their own responsibility or brought face to face with problems which they have not met in their previous experience. For the solution of these problems no general rules can be laid down; each man must work out his own salvation. All that I hope to do is to give a few suggestions from hard-won personal knowledge which may make the road a little easier.

The problems of boundary lie at the foundation of all surveying, for one must know where a line is before he can measure it, and the solution of these problems calls for the same powers of accurate observation and of consecutive and logical thought that are demanded for successful work in any branch of modern science. It is needless to say that the successful surveyor must be accurate in his instrument work and in his computation; yet, if he would really succeed, he must go beyond this. He must add to this the patience to collect all the evidence which can be found bearing upon the case in hand, together with the ability to weigh this evidence to a nicety and to determine clearly the course pointed out by the balance of probability. If, in addition, he possesses enough imagination to cast pleasant lights across the desert of dry details, he should be successful indeed.

The watchwords of the surveyor are Patience and Common Sense.

The vocation of the Civil Engineer has always been invested with a dignity of its own. But it seems to me that of late years, in paying him the honor which is his just due, we are apt to fix a little too wide a gap between him and his humbler brother, the Surveyor. We give engineering the chief attention in our technical schools, but surveying we are wont to relegate to the Freshman class. Yet the profession of the Surveyor deals with one of the oldest and most fundamental facts of human society — the possession and inheritance of land. Fire, flood and earthquake wipe out the greatest works of the engineer, but the land continueth forever.

Curiously enough the Surveyor is isolated in his calling, and therein lie his responsibility and his temptations. The lawyer comes nearest to understanding the work, yet of the actual details of a survey most lawyers are woefully ignorant. The business man who can judge to a hair the fulfillment of a contract has no eye for the shortened line or the shifted landmark.   To the skilled accountant of the bank the traverse sheet is a closed book.   Dishonesty in ordinary business life cannot long be hid and errors in accounts quickly come to light, but the false or faulty survey may pass unchallenged through the years, for few but the Surveyor himself are qualified to judge it.   I maintain that in the hands of the Surveyor, to an exceptional degree, lie the honor of the generations past and the welfare of the generations to come;   in his keeping is the Doomsday Book of his community, and who shall know if he is false to his trust?   Therefore I believe that to every Surveyor who values his honor and has a full sense of his duty the fear of error is a perpetual shadow that darkens the sunlight.

Yet it seems to me that to a man of active mind and high ideals the profession is singularly suited;   for to the reasonable certainty of a modest income must be added the intellectual satisfaction of problems solved, a sense of knowledge and power increasing with the years, the respect of the community, the consciousness of responsibility met and work well done.   It is a profession for men who believe that a man is measured by his work, not by his purse, and to such I commend it.